NELSON MANDELA

"It always seems impossible until it's done."

Frances Ridley

READZONE BOOKS

First published in this edition 2014

ReadZone Books Limited
50 Godfrey Avenue
Twickenham
TW2 7PF
UK

Every attempt has been made by the Publisher to secure appropriate permissions for material reproduced in this book. If there has been any oversight we will be happy to rectify the situation in future editions or reprints. Written submissions should be made to the Publishers.

British Library Cataloguing in Publication Data (CIP) is available for this title.

ISBN 978-1-78322-454-8

Printed in Malta by Melita Press

Developed and Created by Ruby Tuesday Books Ltd
Project Director – Ruth Owen
Designer – Trudi Webb

Photo credits:
Alamy: 28–29; Getty Images: cover, 4–5, 8–9, 11, 12–13, 14–15, 17, 18, 22–23, 25, 27; Public domain: cover, 1, 19, 20–21, 26–27; Shutterstock: 6–7, 16–17 (background), 29.

Acknowledgements
With thanks to Gini Holland, whose writing, research, and personal experience in South Africa made her a valuable resource in assuring the accuracy of the information contained in this book.

Visit our website: www.readzonebooks.com

Contents

Chapter One

Symbol of Hope

In the late 1980s, South Africa was in chaos.

The country was ruled by the National Party. White people had the best land, houses, jobs and education. Black people had been pushed out of their homes. Although black people made up about 90 per cent of the population, they lived on just 13 per cent of the land. They were made to carry **passbooks** to work. They had to leave white areas by sunset. They had no rights, and they were not allowed to vote. This cruel and unfair system was called **apartheid**.

The people were angry. There were **demonstrations** and **riots**. One man's face looked down from the banners. He was the symbol of black suffering. He was also a symbol of hope. His name was Nelson Mandela, and he had been in prison for more than 25 years.

Apartheid

The National Party made apartheid the law in South Africa. This system separated South Africans according to their colour. 'Apartheid' means 'apartness' in Afrikaans, one of the languages of South Africa.

Country Boy

Nelson Mandela was born in 1918 in the village of Mvezo. He was a member of the Thembu tribe of the African Xhosa nation.

Nelson's family owned three thatched huts. One was used for cooking, one for sleeping and one for storage. The family slept on mats and cooked outside over an open fire. Nelson's playground was the pastures and rolling green hills surrounding his home. He fished and swam in the streams and rivers. He made slingshots to bring down birds as they flew overhead. He and his friends used sticks to play fight.

Although the life was simple, Nelson Mandela said:
"It was in that village that I spent some of the happiest years of my boyhood".

After his father had an argument with the Mvezo elders, Nelson's family moved to Qunu. When Nelson was nine his father died of a lung disease, and Nelson went to live with the tribe's chief.

Nelson missed his mother, but he was happy in his new home. He got on well with the chief's son, Justice. He was sent to school and got a good education. The chief held tribal meetings at his home. Every member of the tribe was allowed to speak. The chief listened to everyone before speaking himself. As the sun began to set, the chief summed up what had been said. He tried to find a way for everybody to agree, but he never forced his ideas on people. If all the tribe members could not agree, the chief would hold another meeting.

In his own life, Nelson Mandela tried to lead like the chief – he always tried to listen to everyone.

Troublemaker

'Nelson' was Mandela's English name. His African name was Rolihlahla. The name means 'troublemaker'!

Today, Nelson's grandson, Mandla Mandela, is a tribal chief. Here, he takes part in a traditional dance at his wedding ceremony.

Chapter Three

Rebel

In 1941, the chief arranged marriages for Nelson and Justice. The young men didn't want to marry so they rebelled and ran away to Johannesburg.

In the big city, Nelson had to fend for himself. He got a job as a **clerk** in a law firm. He then went to university and studied law. He was the only black law student at the university.

Friends invited Nelson to African National Congress (ANC) meetings. Nelson had always known he was a member of his tribe. Now he realised that he was also a member of a much larger group – black South Africans. Nelson began working for the ANC. He helped to set up its Youth League.

In Johannesburg, Nelson met Evelyn Mase. They got married in 1944 and started a family.

In 1948, there was an election in South Africa. Only white people were allowed to vote. The National Party won. Its slogan was: *The white man must always remain boss.*

Nelson Mandela, as a young man, wearing the traditional clothes of his tribe.

The ANC

The African National Congress (ANC) was formed in 1912. Its aim was to unite black Africans, and to fight for their rights and their freedom.

Chapter Four

Freedom Fighter

In the 1950s, Nelson juggled home life, work and politics.

Nelson helped the ANC to organise a National Day of Protest on the 26th June, 1950. It was a great success.

In 1952, Nelson and his friend Oliver Tambo opened a law firm called Mandela and Tambo. They helped many black people to fight for justice. Oliver Tambo, like Nelson, was an active member of the ANC. In the same year, the National Party began a crackdown on resistance to apartheid.

Black Africans had to carry passbooks signed by their employers when they travelled outside black areas. They had a curfew that required them to be out of white areas by sunset. In 1952, Nelson and the ANC started a Defiance Campaign. Black people defied these apartheid laws. They didn't obey the curfew.
They refused to carry their passbooks.
They risked being arrested, but there
was massive support for the Campaign.
Membership of the ANC rose from
7000 to 100,000 people.

The Freedom Charter

In 1955, the ANC's beliefs and goals were written down in a document called the Freedom Charter. The charter declared:

South Africa belongs to all who live in it, black and white ... our country will never be prosperous or free until all our people live in brotherhood...

The people in power saw Nelson Mandela as a troublemaker for encouraging people to rebel against apartheid. In 1956, Nelson was arrested for **high treason** and put into prison for several weeks. So were many other leaders of the ANC. The ANC's protests so far had been peaceful. However, the National Party responded to the protests with force. The worst example of this was the Sharpeville Massacre in 1960. Thousands of black people had gathered outside the police station in Sharpeville. They were offering themselves for arrest for not carrying their passbooks. The protest was peaceful, but the police responded by opening fire and killing 69 of the protestors.

This event is often seen as the turning point of the ANC's struggle against apartheid. Nelson argued that the South African government had left the ANC no choice but to meet violence with violence.

Family Troubles

Nelson and Evelyn had three children. Nelson loved his family, but he was too busy to spend time with them. In 1958, Nelson and Evelyn divorced, and he married his second wife, Winnie.

The Sharpeville Massacre

Prisoner

In 1960, the ANC was banned by the National Party. Nelson Mandela went into hiding.

Nelson formed a military group. The group planned to carry out acts of **sabotage**. Their first act was to explode bombs at electric power stations and government offices in major cities in South Africa, including Johannesburg.

The ANC sent Nelson to other countries in Africa and Europe. Nelson took military training and talked to important people who wanted to help the ANC. On his return in 1962, Nelson was arrested and put on trial for sabotage. He was imprisoned on a life sentence.

Spear of the Nation

The military group formed by Nelson Mandela was called 'Umkhonto we Sizwe'. It was also known by the nickname, MK. The name means 'Spear of the Nation'.

Nelson and other ANC members raise their fists in the ANC's salute as they are driven from court to begin their prison sentences.

For the next 27 years, Nelson was a prisoner. For the first 18 years he was imprisoned on Robben Island, a small island off the coast of Cape Town, South Africa.

Nelson and the other prisoners had to do hard labour: digging and cutting rocks in a lime **quarry**. The prisoners were **segregated** by race. Black prisoners got less food than any other group. Nelson was also a **political prisoner**. This meant that he was only allowed one visitor and one letter every six months.

Prison life was harsh, but Nelson and the other ANC prisoners didn't give up hope. Over the years, conditions improved a little on Robben Island. Then, in 1982, Mandela was moved to Pollsmoor Prison. Some of the other ANC leaders were moved there, too.

Nelson Mandela shows photographers how he worked in the quarry during his years as a prisoner on Robben Island.

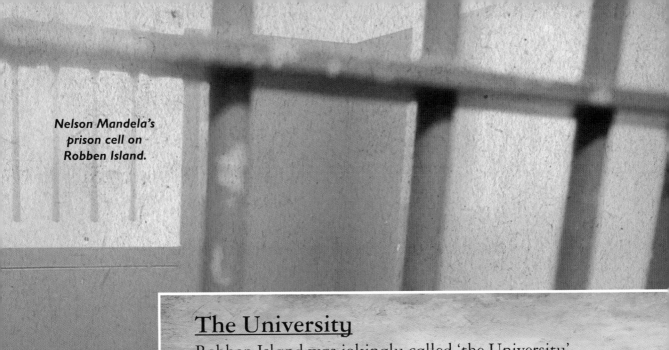

Nelson Mandela's prison cell on Robben Island.

The University

Robben Island was jokingly called 'the University'. Many prisoners studied while they were there. Nelson took a long-distance course with the University of London. He obtained a Bachelor of Laws degree.

Chapter Six

Free Mandela!

In South Africa, black people were still protesting.

On the 16th June, 1976, there was a student protest in Soweto.
The protest became violent and turned into a riot. Hundreds
of people were killed. Over the next few months, the police killed many
more people as they tried to wipe out anti-apartheid protests,
but this only led to more support for the ANC.

In 1980, the headline FREE MANDELA! appeared in the *Johannesburg Sunday Post*. Inside the paper was a petition for people to sign. It asked for the release of Nelson and other political prisoners. The ANC decided to use Nelson's story to give their campaign a 'face'. It was a success. Around the world, people campaigned for the release of Nelson Mandela, and an end to apartheid.

Other countries refused to trade with South Africa and banned the country from taking part in the Olympic Games. Back in South Africa, there were many violent protests.

Student protestors in Soweto.

In 1985, South Africa's president, P. W. Botha, tried to strike a deal — Nelson would be freed if he stopped the violence. Nelson replied: *"Only free men can negotiate. Prisoners cannot enter into contracts."*

In 1986, Nelson began a series of secret meetings with the government. South Africa was getting ready for huge changes.

In August 1989, P. W. Botha resigned as president. F. W. de Klerk took his place. In his first speech as president, de Klerk told South Africa that he wanted peace. He overturned some of the apartheid laws. He also lifted bans on the ANC and other organisations. In 1990, giving in to protests and pressure from around the world, Mr. de Klerk freed Nelson from prison. On the 11th February, 1990, Nelson walked out of the prison gates. The waiting crowds cheered. On television, millions of people around the world saw Nelson lift his right fist in the power salute of his supporters. After 27 years in prison, Nelson Mandela was finally free.

Nelson Mandela walks free from prison. His wife, Winnie, is by his side.

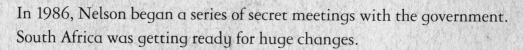

"*I felt – even at the age of seventy-one – that my life was beginning anew.*"

Nelson Mandela

Chapter Seven

World Leader

When Nelson was released from prison, he continued to fight for the end of apartheid.

The ANC agreed to stop the violence and work with the government. But the people were angry. There were still violent clashes between protestors and the police.

This made Nelson and President de Klerk angry. They stopped talking to each other. However, both men realised that they could only bring peace to their country by working together, so they began to meet again.

In 1994, South Africa held its first multi-racial election. The ANC won the election and Nelson Mandela became president of South Africa.

President Mandela helped to unite South Africa's people. He promoted a more positive image of South Africa across the world.

In 1999, Nelson stepped down as president. He retired to Qunu, the village where he grew up.

A Birthday and a Wedding

Nelson divorced his second wife, Winnie, in 1996. In 1998, on his 80th birthday, he married his third wife, Graca Machel.

During South Africa's first multi-racial election, millions of black people queued for hours to vote for the first time.

VOTE FOR JOBS, PEACE AND FREEDOM.

ANC

Nelson Mandela was one of the greatest freedom fighters that the world had ever known. He helped the South African people to defeat the apartheid system, and to rebuild their country. Here are just some of his many achievements.

Nobel Prize Winner

In 1993, Nelson Mandela and F. W. de Klerk were jointly awarded the Nobel Peace Prize for their work in South Africa. The prize celebrates the achievements of people who work towards a more peaceful world.

Sporting Pride

Nelson Mandela encouraged black South Africans to support the South African national rugby team. This helped to bring black and white people together. In 1995, South Africa hosted the Rugby World Cup. The South African team won the trophy! This boosted South Africa's national pride and its status in the rest of the world.

Fighting Against AIDS

Nelson's son, Makgatho, died of **AIDS** in 2005. Nelson set up a charity to make people more aware of AIDS, and to give them information about the disease. The aim was to help prevent the spread of AIDS. The charity is called 46664; this was Nelson's number when he was in prison.

The Elders

In 2008, Nelson Mandela formed 'The Elders'. This group hoped to use their experience and wisdom to help the world solve some of its biggest problems. All the members have been important leaders around the world.

Mandela Day

Nelson Mandela's birthday is now known as 'Mandela Day'. In 2009, a Mandela Day concert was held in New York. It raised funds to help prevent the spread of AIDS.

Chapter Eight

Goodbye, Madiba

In summer 2010, South Africa hosted the World Cup.
To the cheers of a huge crowd, Nelson Mandela
attended the closing ceremony at FNB Stadium,
also known as Soccer City, in Johannesburg.
It would be his last public appearance.

On the 5th December, 2013, Nelson Mandela died. He was 95.
In South Africa, and around the world, people mourned the death
of this extraordinary man.

Five days later, a memorial service was held at FNB Stadium.
Over 100 world leaders, as well as thousands of ordinary South
Africans, attended the event. Together they remembered and
celebrated the man whom many South Africans call Madiba.
On the 15th December, Nelson was buried in his home village of Qunu.

Nelson's life began simply. He went on, however, to free his people
from apartheid and become president of his country. Loved
and respected around the world, Nelson Rolihlahla Mandela
will never be forgotten.

*U.S. President
Barack Obama
speaking
at Nelson's
memorial
service*

Madiba

The name 'Madiba' is Nelson's clan name. It is used as a sign of respect and affection.

Thousands of mourners attended Nelson Mandela's memorial service.

Glossary

AIDS Short for acquired immune deficiency syndrome. AIDS is often a deadly disease as it prevents the body from defending itself against illness and infection.

apartheid A word in the Afrikaans language meaning 'apartness'. Apartheid is a system of racial segregation and discrimination.

clerk In a law firm, a person who helps lawyers carry out research and perform other tasks.

demonstration A public gathering or march to protest against something or to show feelings about a political issue.

high treason The crime of betraying or being disloyal to one's country.

passbook A booklet that black South Africans were required to carry and have signed by white employers in order for them to move about in white-only areas.

political prisoner A person imprisoned for his or her political beliefs or actions.

quarry A place, usually a large, deep pit, from which stone, gravel, or some other material is removed.

riot A disturbance caused by a crowd, usually one that is expressing its anger in a violent way.

sabotage The act of destroying or damaging something on purpose, usually for a political or military reason.

segregated Divided, separated, or set apart from others, often on the basis of race.

Index